A Great Round Wonder

My Book of the World

BY **Shelley Tanaka**

ILLUSTRATED BY **Debi Perna**

Douglas & McIntyre
Toronto Vancouver Buffalo

Text copyright © 1993 by Shelley Tanaka
Illustrations copyright © 1993 by Debi Perna
First U.S. Publication 1994

The publisher gratefully acknowledges the assistance of
the Canada Council.

Douglas & McIntyre Ltd.
585 Bloor Street West
Toronto, Ontario M6G 1K5

Canadian Cataloguing in Publication Data

Tanaka, Shelley.
      A great round wonder : my book of the world

ISBN 1-55054-213-3

1. Environmental protection – Juvenile literature.
2. Man – Influence on nature – Juvenile literature.
3. Earth – juvenile literature.   I. Perna, Debi.
II. Title.

TD170.15.T36 1993   j363.7   C93-093128-9

Library of Congress
Cataloguing-in-Publication Data
is available.

Special thanks to Badie Boctor

Design by Michael Solomon
Printed and bound in Hong Kong

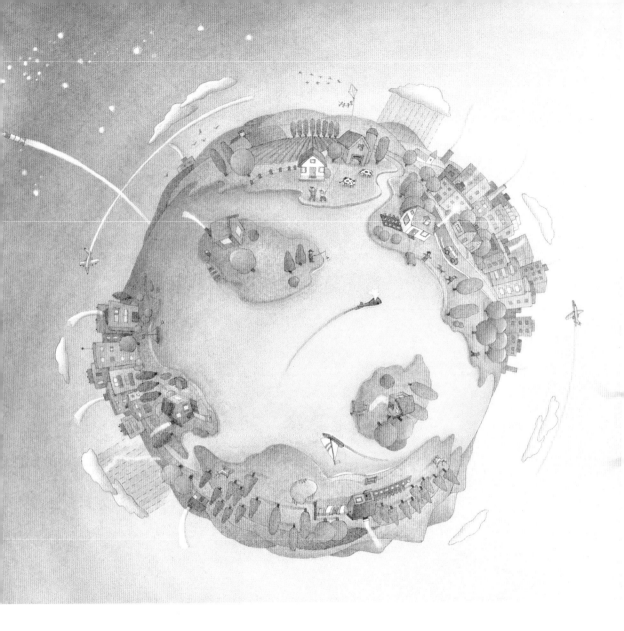

I see a great round wonder rolling through space . . .
I see the shaded part on one side where the sleepers are
   sleeping, and the sunlit part on the other side . . .
I see distant lands, as real and near to the inhabitants
   of them as my land is to me.

From "Salut au monde!" by Walt Whitman

Look out your window . . .

What do you see? Your apartment balcony? Your yard? A street full of cars and trucks? Your schoolground?

What you see is your **environment**. The environment is everything around you. Your bedroom is part of your environment. So is your whole house and the air around it.

But your environment also stretches far beyond what you can see. It goes on and on, around the whole world.

As our planet, Earth, rolls through space, billions of people are going about their busy days. Babies are crying and sleeping.

Children are playing and going to school, and parents are working. Birds, animals and insects of all kinds are making their homes and searching for food. Tall trees and delicate grasses are reaching up to the sun and waving in the wind.

Everywhere, the Earth is

bursting with the lives of countless creatures that make the planet their home.

There are three ingredients that make it possible for the Earth to give life to so many things. There's the **air** all around us, the **water** in the rivers and oceans, and the **soil** under our feet. Without these three ingredients, we could not live. Neither could the birds, animals, bugs and plants.

We all need clean air to breathe and clean water to drink. We need healthy soil to grow the food we eat.

Air to breathe . . .

Everyone knows you can't live without air. People need air to breathe. So do cows, cats, birds, bugs, and even plants. But most of us don't think too much about air. Why should we, when we can't even see it?

In the winter air feels cold. In the summer it feels hot. But most of the time air just hangs around, filling up space.

Air looks invisible, but it really contains tiny specks of dust, dirt and smoke. When there are too many dirt specks floating around, the air is polluted. **Pollution** hurts the plants and trees. It hurts people, too.

Where does air pollution come from? Big factories add a lot of dirt to the air. So do the millions of cars that we drive to school and work every day.

The word **smog** is made of two words: **sm**oke + f**og**. Since cars make our air smelly and dirty, maybe we should call them stinkmobiles!

Air is made of many different gases. Two important ones are **oxygen** and **carbon dioxide**.

When people and animals breathe in, they use the oxygen that is in the air. We need oxygen to stay alive. When we breathe out, we blow out carbon dioxide.

Plants and trees use air, too. But they take in carbon dioxide. Then they give out the oxygen that we need to breathe.

The smoke that comes out of factory chimneys and car tailpipes can turn into **smog**. This is one kind of air pollution that you can actually see. When you drive into a big city, sometimes you'll see smog hanging over the buildings like a grayish yellow fuzz.

Factory smoke and car smoke contain invisible gases. Some of these gases, such as carbon dioxide, are a normal part of the air. But others were never meant for people and plants to breathe.

Now factories and cars are adding too many gases to the air. This is causing the **Greenhouse Effect**.

When the weather is cool, gardeners can grow plants in a special house built of glass. This house is called a greenhouse. The sun shines in through the glass, and part of the sunlight changes to heat. But the glass stops this heat from getting out again. Inside the greenhouse the air is warmer than it is outside.

The gases from car and factory smoke hang over the Earth like the glass on a greenhouse. The sunlight shines down and turns into heat. But the wall of gases stops the heat from bouncing back up into the sky. Many scientists think this is making the air around the Earth warmer than normal. People call this **global warming**.

Some people think it would be great to have more days of swimming weather. Maybe we could wear shorts all year long!

But weird things could happen if the Earth got even a bit warmer. The weather could change all over the world. Some farms might turn into deserts, like giant sandboxes. At the North and South poles huge chunks of ice might start to melt. The extra water would fill the oceans and make them overflow. Seaside cities might be drowned in water. Warm places could become too hot to live in or grow food plants in.

Most people can't even notice global warming, because it is happening very slowly. But it is still taking place too fast for the Earth to handle easily.

We can't just sit around and wait to see what happens. That's why factories must stop putting so many gases into the air. That's why we must all stop driving our cars so much.

Keeping smoke and gases out of the air isn't our only problem.

The Earth is covered by a thick blanket of air called the **atmosphere**. Very high up is a special layer of atmosphere called the **ozone layer**. It is like a shield that stops some of the sun's harmful rays from hitting the Earth.

If the ozone layer weren't there, we would all get bad sunburns, or even a sickness called skin cancer. Some of our food plants would be ruined.

Scientists have discovered that the ozone layer is getting thinner in some places. There is a thin spot over the South Pole, where the penguins live. There is another one over Canada's Far North. This means that more of the sun's rays are getting through to the Earth.

CFC stands for chlorofluorocarbon. No wonder everyone uses a short form instead!

Most scientists think chemicals are causing the ozone layer to get thinner. People have made these chemicals. Some are used when factories make some plastic foams (the kind in egg cartons or hamburger boxes). They are also used in refrigerators and air-conditioners and some spray cans that hold things like furniture polish.

Some of the chemicals are called **CFCs.** When CFCs get into the air, they float up into the atmosphere. Then they break down the ozone.

When people found out that some plastic foams and spray cans were bad for the ozone, they didn't want to buy them anymore. So most factories stopped using CFCs.

But refrigerators and air-conditioners are still a big problem (especially car air-conditioners). One day we will all be able to buy refrigerators that aren't bad for the ozone layer. In the meantime, shouldn't we think twice before we turn on our air-conditioners?

Water to drink . . .

What's so precious about water? Why do we have to worry about it? When we're thirsty, we just turn on the tap to get a drink. When we want to wash the dishes or take a bath, we fill up the sink or bathtub. Water always comes out of the tap.

We expect our water to be clean and safe to drink. But where does it come from? Where does the dirty water go after it disappears down the drain?

Our water comes from nearby lakes or rivers, or from pools that lie deep under the ground. Pipes take the water into our houses so we can use it.

If you live in the country, your used water probably goes into a septic tank, which removes the dirt. If you live in the city, pipes carry your dirty water to a sewage plant that cleans it.

After the used water is cleaned, sometimes it goes back into the same lakes that it came from. Sometimes it sinks into the ground. Then it is called **groundwater**. Some of the groundwater is taken up by plants and trees. Some of it runs into rivers and lakes. And some of it dribbles back into the underground pools. Then we use it again and again.

So when we get "fresh" water out of the tap, it really isn't fresh at all. The Earth doesn't make new water. We just use the same old water over and over.

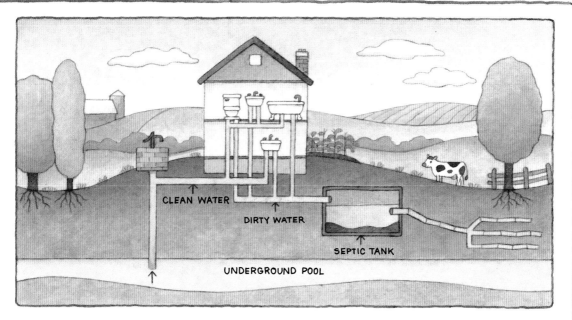

CLEAN WATER

DIRTY WATER

SEPTIC TANK

UNDERGROUND POOL

Of course, we try to make sure the water is safe to drink before we use it again. We add chemicals to kill germs and get rid of the bad tastes and smells. But it is still all the same water.

The world has been reusing its water for a long time, so why is this such a big problem now? Part of the problem is that there are more and more people on the Earth using the same amount of water. What is even worse, some poisons are getting into our water.

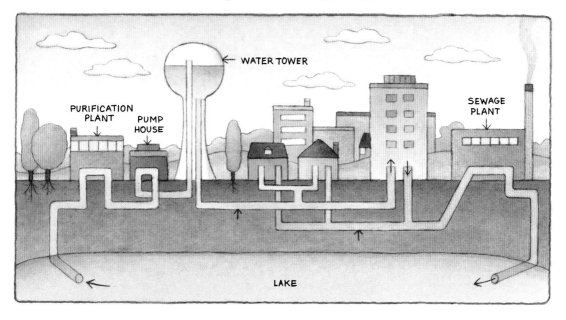

WATER TOWER

PURIFICATION PLANT

PUMP HOUSE

SEWAGE PLANT

LAKE

You would never want to drink paint, car oil, oven cleaner or bug spray. You wouldn't want to take a bath in a tub of the chemicals that factories use when they make things. But all these things get into our water.

When we pour paint or cleaners down the drain, they run into our lakes and rivers. When car oil spills on the ground, it sinks down into the groundwater. When we throw old batteries into the garbage dump, the rain can wash poisonous metals out of them into under-ground pools. After factories make things, leftover chemicals are sometimes thrown away in the used water.

Just about everything that we put on the ground eventually gets into the groundwater. The salt that we sprinkle on the road to melt the snow. The **fertilizers** that we put on the soil to help plants grow. The **herbicides** that we spray on our lawns to kill dandelions. The **pesticides** that we put on plants to kill potato bugs and cabbage worms.

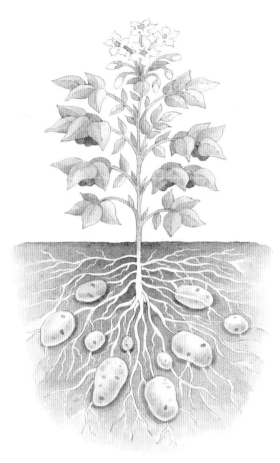

Once some of these harmful things are in the water, they can stay there for a long, long time. Tiny amounts are taken up by plants and trees, including our food plants.

If we're not careful, before long we will have very little water fit to drink. So what can we do?

We can start by getting rid of unhealthy chemicals more carefully. Leftover cleaners and paints and used batteries can be taken to special places where they are thrown out safely.

But it would be even better if we stopped using some of these things in the first place. We can use sand instead of salt on our roads in the winter. We can make our own cleaners at home using safe ingredients, instead of buying harsh chemical ones at the store. We can use rechargeable batteries instead of the kind you have to throw out. We can stop being fussy about eating apples with little bruises or worm holes on them, so farmers won't think they have to use so many pesticides.

Our oceans are becoming polluted, too. Some factories just pour their dirty water right into the sea. Some throw tins full of chemicals into the ocean. When the tins get rusty and fall apart, the chemicals inside them leak into the water.

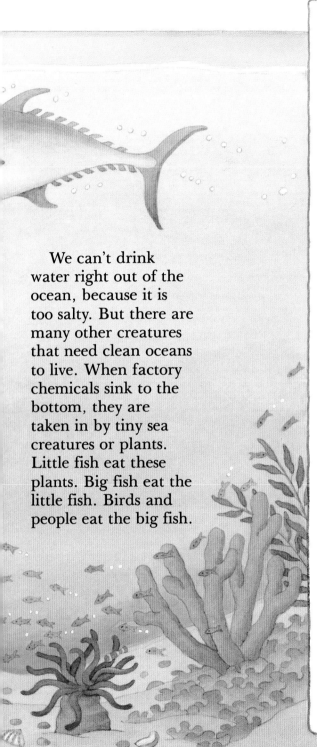

We can't drink water right out of the ocean, because it is too salty. But there are many other creatures that need clean oceans to live. When factory chemicals sink to the bottom, they are taken in by tiny sea creatures or plants. Little fish eat these plants. Big fish eat the little fish. Birds and people eat the big fish.

Every time we go to the gas station, we fill up the car with gasoline. Gasoline is made from oil. We also use oil in the furnaces that heat some of our homes.

A lot of our oil comes from countries that lie far across the ocean. The oil is carried in supertankers, huge ships that can be as long as four football fields.

Supertankers can have accidents, the same way cars do. A tanker can crash against a rock, or against another ship. Sometimes the crash makes a hole in the ship's belly. If this happens, the oil inside rushes out.

This is called an **oil spill**. The oil floats on top of the water like a thick layer of guck. Sea birds get covered in it. Dolphins and whales can't breathe. The seashore becomes covered with shiny black slime.

It is impossible to clean up all the oil, and it takes a long time for the ocean to become healthy again.

We need smaller oil tankers with extra-strong bottoms that can't be broken. We need to stop using so much oil.

Acid rain is another water problem.

Some factories and power stations burn coal to make them run. Cars burn gasoline.

The gases from the coal smoke and gasoline smoke float up into the air, where they mix with the water in the rain clouds. Some of these gases make the water in the clouds acidic or sour, like lemon juice.

The wind can blow these clouds far away, to countrysides filled with lakes and forests. When the clouds get too full and heavy, the acid rain falls out. Sometimes the rain falls in other countries, far away from the factories that caused the problem in the first place.

When the acid rainwater is soaked up by trees and plants, they may stop growing. When the rain fills up the lakes, the fish, tadpoles,

water snakes and lake plants all die. The mosquitoes and other bugs go away. Then there is nothing for the birds to eat, so they leave, too. Before long, the lakes and the environment around them are dead and empty.

Acid rain is everybody's problem, because the wind blows the rain clouds far away from the factories that are making the smoke. Now neighbors are starting to work together. Some factories want to stop burning coal. Some are trying to clean out their coal smoke so it doesn't add harmful gases to the air. We should cheer for these companies.

We must all stop driving our cars so much. Then fewer harmful gases will get into the air. We should also find safer, cleaner ways to make our cars go, so we don't have to use as much gasoline.

Soil to grow our food . . .

Everyone knows soil is the brown stuff that plants and trees grow in. It's just dirt, isn't it? It gets under our fingernails when we dig a hole in the ground to plant a tree or make a tunnel. We try not to bring it into the house. Grownups like to cover it up with lawn or flowers or cement patios.

But should we really call soil dirt? What exactly is it, and why is it so important?

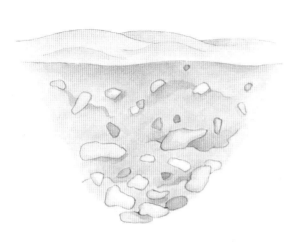

To grow, plants need food and water, just like people do. Plants use humus to get the minerals they need for food. They take in water from the soil. Soil that is full of organic humus and clean water is healthy soil.

Soil is made of two things. One part is rock. Sometimes the rock is in big chunks. Sometimes it comes in small pebbles or very tiny pieces called sand.

Plants don't grow well in soil that is mostly rock.

The other part of soil is **humus**. Humus is **organic** material — plants and animals that were once alive. When the plants and animals die, they **rot**, or decay. They shrivel up and fall apart.

Almost everything we eat comes from plants, or from animals that feed on plants. Apples and bananas come from trees. Peanuts for your peanut butter come from peanut plants. Crackers and bread are made from grain plants.

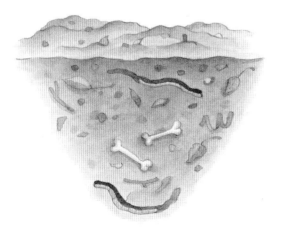

Pigs and cows and chickens eat plants, too. So when we eat pork chops or hamburgers or ice cream or eggs, we are also eating plants.

People and animals need to eat plants to live. Plants need healthy soil to grow. That's why soil is so important.

There are many ways soil can be ruined. One way is to take all the humus out of it. If we keep growing plants in the same soil without adding organic material such as manure and compost, all the humus is used up. Then there is only rock left. The land becomes a sandy desert where nothing can grow.

Many farmers say it is too much trouble to add manure and compost to the soil. Instead, they use factory-made **fertilizer**. When the rain washes the fertilizer into the ground, it gets into our drinking water. Fertilizer helps plants grow, but nobody wants to drink it.

Soil can become polluted by the things that people throw on top of it or bury under it, like **garbage**.

Every day, we throw out piles and piles of dirty diapers, used paper towels, gum wrappers, old shampoo bottles, stinky meat bones, jars and paper. We stuff it all into trash cans or plastic bags. Soon a truck comes and takes it out of sight. Then we stop worrying about it.

But where does the garbage go?

In some places the garbage goes to an **incinerator**. This is a huge furnace that burns the garbage in a very hot fire.

But incinerators don't get rid of everything.

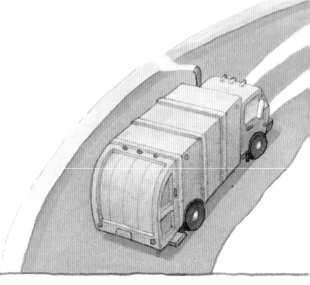

For instance, plastic containers, glues and paper are made with chemicals. When we burn these things, the chemicals can stay in the smoke from the fire. The smoke goes up the chimney, and the chemicals can get into the air. They get mixed into the clouds, and the rain washes them into the water that we drink. They sink into the soil where we grow our food plants.

We can't get rid of all the incinerators. But we can try to stop buying things that are made with harmful chemicals. That would be a big help.

Some places bury their garbage in a huge hole called a **landfill**. Landfill is a nice name for **dump**. When the hole is full, bulldozers cover the garbage up so it looks like part of the land again. But underneath it's still garbage — the same diapers and bottles and plastic bags just covered up with soil.

We are running out of places to bury our garbage. Do you want a dump near your town? Everyone knows garbage can smell. Everyone also knows that all that nasty garbage water will soon get washed into the lakes and wells that give them their drinking water.

This is why there is a **garbage crisis**. Too much garbage, and no place to put it.

Many cities are trying to keep garbage out of dumps by **recycling**. They make new bottles out of old bottles, or new paper out of old paper. Some people are trying to **reuse** some of their things. They give away their old clothes and toys instead of throwing them out.

If you dug up garbage that your grandparents buried, what would it look like? The apple cores and chicken bones would probably be gone, because they are organic. They rot and become part of the soil again. But you would still be able to dig up old shoes, jars, cans and spoons that looked the same as they did when your grandparents buried them.

Some garbage sits around for a long, long time.

Recycling and reusing are both good. But the best way to help is to **reduce** by not buying things that have to be thrown out.

This means using cloth diapers instead of throwaway ones, using dishrags instead of paper towels, and writing on both sides of a piece of paper, even though it would be nicer to get a fresh piece. It means taking your juice to school in a Thermos instead of buying a juice box and straw.

And it means not buying something that you know you won't really want in a week or so, like the plastic toys you get in gum machines.

Reducing sounds hard, for grownups and kids. Who's going to wash all those diapers and dishrags? Will shopping trips be even more boring if you can't buy a small toy wrapped in shiny plastic? Who's going to remember to take an old plastic container to the store every time you need more raisins?

But think how great it would be if everybody did this. What a difference it would make.

So the next time you walk past a gum machine and don't stick your money in, be happy. You're doing something good for the planet.

Your planet.

Our poor soil is in trouble in another way, too.

Every year there are more and more people in the world. These people all need a place to live, so cities get bigger. We need more roads to take everyone to work and school. We need bigger farms to grow more food. We have to build more factories to make cars and clothes and toys for everyone.

In some countries, people are cutting down **rainforests** for houses, food and jobs. But the rainforests are important. They are filled with very old, very tall trees. The trees give us things we need, such as rubber, nuts and many medicines. The rainforests are also home to millions of different animals and plants.

When the trees are cut down, the animals lose their usual home, or **habitat**. Without a home, the animals begin to disappear. This means they are **endangered**. If they continue to disappear, they will all die and be gone from the Earth forever. Then they will be **extinct**, like the dinosaurs.

The rainforests aren't the only forests that are disappearing. All over the world people are cutting down millions of trees.

We need trees. They keep the air clean and healthy. They help reduce the Greenhouse Effect. They give out the oxygen that people and animals must have.

Trees also shade the ground so the soil doesn't dry out. Their roots stop the humus in the soil from blowing or washing away.

Let's plant lots of new trees and protect the old ones. Let's help the poorer countries so they don't have to cut down so many forests.

Looking after trees is just one more way to look after the soil, and our world.

There's no such thing as far away..

We sometimes talk about the air, water and soil as if they were separate things. But they are really all connected.

When the sun heats up the lakes and oceans, tiny invisible drops of water rise up into the air. The drops gather together to make clouds. When the drops get too heavy, they fall as rain. The rain sinks into the soil. It falls into the oceans, lakes and rivers. Then the drops rise up into the air again.

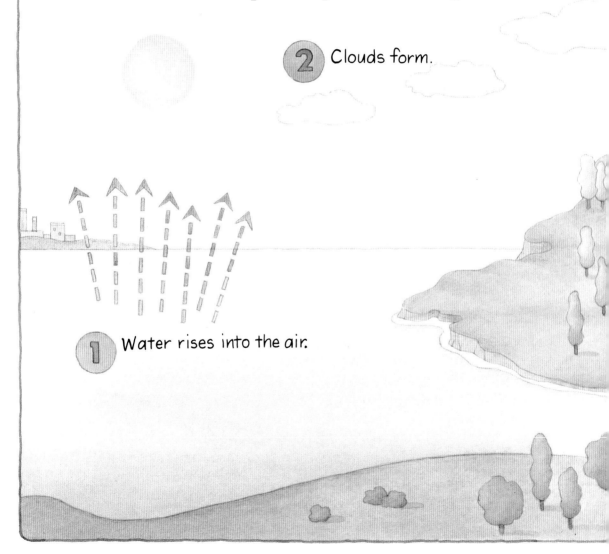

2 Clouds form.

1 Water rises into the air.

3 Rain falls.

This is how the Earth's water moves from one place to another. We call this the **water cycle**. A cycle is something that goes around and around, happening over and over again. Pollution that is in one part of the cycle eventually gets into all the other parts.

4 Water flows back to the sea.

The **food cycle** is another cycle. Plants take food they need out of the soil. Animals eat the plants. When animals and plants die, their bodies rot and decay to make food for the soil so more plants can grow and more animals can feed on them. This is how nature turns waste into something it can use again. This is how the Earth looks after itself.

The Earth's cycles aren't working as well as they used to. People have put things into the air, water and soil that the Earth doesn't know how to deal with — things like plastic bags and smoke from cars. Pollution things.

When we burn or bury something, or flush it down the drain, it doesn't go away. It stays around. It gets into everything.

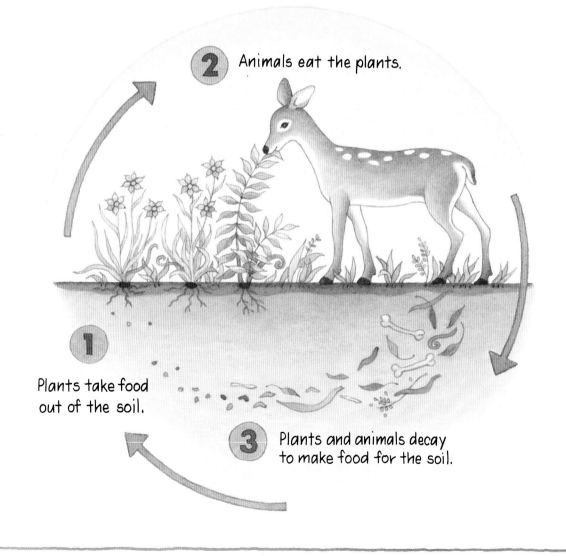

2 Animals eat the plants.

1 Plants take food out of the soil.

3 Plants and animals decay to make food for the soil.

There are no separate parts to the Earth. Everything is connected, the same way your legs and arms are attached to the rest of your body. When you have the stomach flu, often your whole body feels sick. The Earth is like that, too. It is one huge living, breathing body. What happens in one part of the world happens to all of us.

It's hard to think of the Earth this way, because it is such a big place. The rainforest jungles, filled with snakes and jaguars, seem very far away. It's hard to worry about the ozone layer because it's invisible. It's hard to think about our garbage once it has been picked up and carried out of sight.

But there's no such thing as far away or out of sight.

The Island That Took Care of Itself

Somewhere in the middle of the ocean, there was a little island. The island looked very bare, covered only by sand. There were no trees. There were no hills or lakes or rivers.

But the island wasn't as empty as it looked. Enough rain and snow fell to fill ponds with fresh water. Between the humps of sand there were green grasses and cranberry bushes for birds to eat. There was even enough grass and water to feed a small herd of wild horses that ran free on the island.

Although there wasn't much on it, the island looked after itself. The horses grew up and had more and more babies, until it looked as though there would not be enough grass to feed them all. But then an extra-cold winter came along. The older and weaker animals died, but their dead bodies rotted and decayed and made the soil rich so the grass could grow well.

The island managed just fine this way for a long, long time.

Then one day, people found the island and decided to move in.

They didn't want to eat horses, so they brought rabbits over on a ship and let them loose. The rabbits had so many babies that soon there were too many for the people to eat. The rabbits ate up the plants and grass, until there was little left for the people or the horses.

So the people brought over cats to eat all the rabbits. The cats did this, but then they started having kittens. Soon there were wild cats all over the island. They were as much of a nuisance as the rabbits. And the people didn't want to eat the cats.

So the people brought over foxes to eat the cats. But the foxes started to eat the birds, too.

With few birds around to eat them, grasshoppers started to eat up all the plants.

Finally, the people decided enough was enough. They took out their guns and shot all the foxes. Then they packed their bags and went away themselves.

Soon the birds came back and started eating grasshoppers again. The plants grew back. With no rabbits, cats, foxes or people, the island was back to the way it was in the first place.

Once again, it could look after itself.

How did all this happen?

How did our Earth get so messed up? If people are so smart, how could they cause all these problems?

Things got this way partly because people can be too smart for their own good.

Back in the old days, when your great-great-grandparents were growing up, people had two main worries: staying warm and getting enough to eat. They had to chop wood and build fires to keep warm. They grew their own food. There were no cars, so people had to walk a long way to get to school or to a friend's house.

There were no electric lights, televisions, telephones or refrigerators. No paper towels, potato chips, popsicles or microwave dinners.

Life was hard work, but the air and water and soil were clean and healthy.

Then people started to use their brains to make their lives easier. They invented pumps to bring water out of the ground so they didn't have to pull it up in a bucket. They invented washing machines so they didn't have to scrub the dirt off their clothes by hand.

Then someone discovered electricity. Someone invented the telephone. The first car was invented. Factories were built to make all the new things people were beginning to use. Power stations were built to make electricity. These power stations needed fuel to burn, so huge amounts of coal, gas and oil were dug out of the ground.

Inventions became even more clever and complicated. When certain insects began to eat too many food plants, scientists invented a fancy new poison, or pesticide, to kill them. People discovered that a metal called uranium could be used to make electricity. This was known as **nuclear energy**, and everyone thought we could now have all the electricity we wanted.

People didn't have to work as hard as before, so they lived longer. Scientists discovered new medicines so people didn't get sick as often. More babies were born. The **population** began to grow. Every year there were more people on the Earth.

Everyone thought this was great, because it meant more people to buy and make things. The idea that it is good to make and buy more and more things is called **consumerism**.

Having all these things meant people could have a comfortable **lifestyle**. Dishwashers washed their dishes. Electric washing machines cleaned their laundry. There were new inventions so people could have fun while machines were doing all their work — television sets, CD players, VCRs, satellite dishes, Walkmans, snow-mobiles, sports cars, Nintendo.

Factories became bigger and more powerful so they could make more things. People drove around in big cars, just for fun. Some families bought two cars, or a motor boat. Factories dumped their garbage into the ocean. They thought the oceans were so big that the stuff would just disappear. Families didn't worry about their garbage, either, because there was a lot of space to bury it.

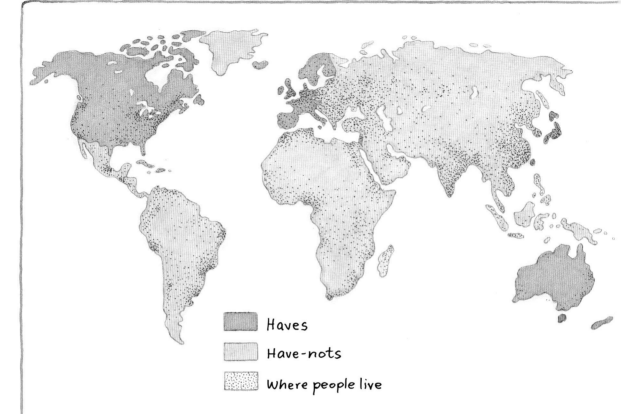

	Haves
	Have-nots
	Where people live

But the Earth couldn't keep up with it all. The oceans were big, but they weren't big enough to hold all the garbage that people threw into them. Factory smokestacks started to put so much smoke into the air that it became unsafe to breathe. Many forests were cut down to make room for farms and cities, so some animals and birds had no place left to live.

People began to use some of their clever inventions unwisely. Nuclear energy caused some complicated safety problems, and no one could figure out how to solve them completely. Pesticides were killing good insects as well as the "bad" ones. There were more and more cars on the roads, and people loved them so much that they wanted to drive them everywhere — even to the corner store!

All these things have happened mainly in the rich countries of the world. The people in these countries are **haves**. We have enough food to eat, clothes to keep us warm, money to buy the things we need.

But most of the people in the world are **have-nots**. There are have-nots in every country, but many of them live in the poor countries of the world. In these countries, the land and weather often aren't good for farming, so people can't always grow enough food to feed themselves. They often don't have hospitals and doctors to take care of the sick. A lot of babies and children die or are unhealthy.

These people need to live better lives. They would like to have cars and dishwashers, too. But this is hard because the rich countries are using up most of the world's **resources** — the food, and the things that make **energy**, such as oil and gas.

This isn't fair. Sooner or later, the haves will have to share with the have-nots. And everyone in the world will have to take better care of our planet.

What happens in one place soon moves into other places. The smoke from the barbecue next door can float into your yard. The pollution from factories in another country can get into the rain water that falls on the trees in your park. When a tanker spills its load of oil, the wind can push the oil onto the beach where you like to swim. The ash and smoke from a large volcano can change the weather halfway around the world.

Our world is really a very small place. What happens in one spot happens to all of us.

What's the good news?

Pollution, garbage crisis, global warming, acid rain. These words sound like such bad news. Why can't we just buy what we want, have a good time, be happy?

Because if we pretend there is no problem, things will just get worse. But if we find out what these words mean, we can turn the bad news into good news.

Solar energy, wind power, organic farming, composting, the 3 Rs. These are just some of the ways people are starting to solve the problems with our environment.

The sun is a big hot, fiery ball, full of energy. We can use sunshine to make heat and electricity. This is called **solar energy**. Right now, most of the ways we make electricity and heat hurt the Earth in some way. But solar energy doesn't pollute the air, water or the soil. Engineers are even inventing cars and airplanes that run on the energy from sunlight!

We must cheer on the scientists who are working with solar energy. If we do, one day we may all use the sun to heat our homes and run our factories.

The wind can make things go, too, the same way it blows a sailboat across the water. **Wind power** uses the wind to make electricity. Wind power doesn't pollute the Earth, either. Some places in the world already have wind farms — big fields filled with rows and rows of windmills. These farms can make electricity to heat our water, run pumps and light up our homes.

Some people who grow our food plants are becoming **organic farmers**. They grow fruits and vegetables without using factory-made fertilizers or pesticides. Organic food is healthier for people to eat. It is better for the soil and water.

by walking or biking to school instead of asking for a ride.

Doing these things will give our Earth time to get better. They are **environmentally friendly**. Some people call environmentally friendly things **green**, because green is the color of healthy plants.

All over the world, green businesses, government leaders, teachers, parents and children are working together. They are cleaning up the air, water and soil. They are changing the way we treat our planet.

GREEN!

And all over, families are following the **3Rs — reducing, reusing** and **recycling**. Maybe you have a compost pile at home or at school, too. Or perhaps you **conserve energy** by turning off the lights when you leave a room or

The Earth is a complicated living machine, full of many mysteries. We don't know exactly how it works. We don't know how much harm we can do before it stops working the way it should.

Imagine that the Earth is one gigantic spider web, where every string is connected to the rest. If you cut one string, no one may notice. If you cut several strings, the web will start to droop. And if you keep cutting, one day you will cut one string too many. Then the web will fall apart completely.

Our Earth's web is drooping. It's time to start fixing the strings.

Every time you recycle a juice

can, or carry a bowl of vegetable peels to the compost, you are mending a string in the web. Every time you walk instead of taking the car, you are helping to put the Earth's web back together.

If we each do a little bit, together we can make the Earth healthy again.

After all, we're all in this together. We all breathe the same air. We drink the same water and grow our food on the same soil.

We are all part of the same planet.

It's the only planet we have.